## DEDICATION

To all the men and women, alive and dead, who answered our nation's call to serve in Vietnam; to all those who have forgotten their stories and to those who would rather forget but can't. This is a short story, my story. I am proud to have served with Marines.

Semper Fidelis

# 1st Lt. Lee Suydam

As if it were yesterday....an old fat man remembers his youth as a Marine in Vietnam.

Before 2nd Battalion, First Marines (2/1) left the Danang area and headed to Quang Tri, the Battalion was perimetered in an abandoned village called Phong Loc. Our purpose was to prevent enemy forces from bringing rockets into range of the air base at Da Nang. I joined 2/1 as a newly commissioned 2nd Lieutenant and was assigned as Platoon Commander of the third platoon of Echo Company.

It was in Phong Ngu where our platoon sized missions roved for three to four days at a time. It was

3

a place for snipers, booby traps, occasional firefights and ambush. Each night we would set up in a village, either that or sleep on top of graves in the rice paddies, but after nightfall, we would slip away and set up again under cover of darkness. Invariably, the place we left was fragged during the night. Once during daylight, I left a squad hidden in a village, walked out to Highway 1 and doubled back by a more northern route. The Viet Cong (VC) closed in behind us and our hidden squad was able to ambush successfully, capturing one VC which we took to Battalion HQ.

Highway 1 was the north-south artery that ran from Hanoi to Saigon along the eastern side of Vietnam. As you traveled south along Route 1, you passed through Dien Ban, a French built city-market with walls and eventually crossed the Song Cau Lau. This great river is formed by the merger of the great Song Ky Lam and the lesser Song Chiem Sun. These two rivers run close together forming a landmass between them that we called Go Noi Island because of the abandoned village there, Go Noi. The island ran east and west for eighteen kilometers and was four kilometers at its widest point. Echo Company had been there before and there were many old stories circulating among the troops about the horrors to be found there. Abandoned by the civilian population, the area was filled with trench works and fortifications and had the signs of a battlefield from the many clashes of adversaries. The Island was reportedly a VC Regimental Headquarters. Echo Company was to acquire the island by stealth in

5

the darkness and then root out the enemy.

Before jumping off, we spent some time in the city of Duy Xuyen (pronounced Dewy Schwen). There was a large market in the center of town where we bought pineapples. I remember the excitement caused when three fishermen rolled in a freshly caught shark, about six-foot long, draped over their bicycle into the crowded market. The shark was cut loose to flop onto the cobble stone pavement whereupon the fishermen immediately began to butcher it. Women rushed forward holding out banana leaves upon which to receive a slice or some innard part. There was loud cackling and bartering of all manner; none of which we understood.

We approached Go Noi Island from the south sometime after midnight by wading across the Song Chiem Sun. The water was cold and neck deep but no current. Third platoon was last to cross. Echo turned left upon entering the Island while we (3rd platoon) turned right and formed a line along the river. We set up and waited the dawn.

Before dawn arrived, my troops saw a man in a round basket boat paddling in circles in the area where we had just crossed the river. He stayed there for an hour, and then he vanished. As dawn came, three VC walked into our perimeter and stepped on some of our sleeping troops. These VC were the first three casualties of our visit. Moments later, a VC opened a tunnel entrance in the middle of the Company Command Post (CP). He was summarily

7

dispatched. The four dead VC confirmed that we had successfully entered their midst undiscovered and that we were waking up among them.

The Company CP was about 300 meters to our west circled by the middle platoon. At some point, I believe either the first or second day, a chopper landed with mail and C-rations. I dispatched a fire team to walk the 300 meters down to the CP and return with our share. At the last minute, the Company Commander (CO) radioed for Platoon Commanders to assemble. So, I got up and followed the fire team to the CP. I didn't think to take the radioman. It had been quiet for a long time and it was only 300 meters away. On our way down, we saw four ARVN troops (South Vietnamese Army) along a tree line to our north with their colorful Boy Scout-like neckerchiefs. They gave us a friendly wave and we all waved back. Our comment at the time was, "I didn't know there were ARVN troops on this mission." I thought no more of it. ARVN troops among our own were a common situation. These men not only looked ARVN but also carried the typical WW II era weapons furnished by the US. I thought so little of it that I didn't even mention the sighting to Captain Pratt. I had 10 weeks of PLC, 8 weeks of Parris Island, 12 weeks of Infantry Training, 8 weeks of OCS, and 21 weeks of The Basis School for Officers. That's 59 weeks of Marine Training. You would think they would have prepared me for everything. But, I was young and inexperienced. My eyes were soon to be opened.

We had our meeting, we talked about the strange events of the first morning, and we were on our way back to our platoon perimeter. Suddenly, the world was shooting at us. We dropped the mail and C-rats in the trail and fell into a trench along the right side the trail. I pulled my 45 and aimed it forward. The lead man, Sargent Miller, had jumped left off the trail, so I was the most forward one in the trench. My 45-cal. pistol was like a popgun compared to the opposing firepower, but it was the only thing I had.

There was clearly a Browning Automatic Rifle (BAR) booming down the trail and the mailbag danced a jig each time he opened up. The C-rats boxes were being perforated as peach juice and beans oozed out and ran down the sides. There was also an M-79 grenade launcher trying to find our range and several other automatic and semi-automatic small arms popping over our heads. I distinctly heard the chirping of a US M1 carbine. Suddenly, the trooper behind me took a round in his left lung, high, near his collarbone. I looked forward and saw the side of the trench explode and knew they were firing down the trench. (At the time, I thought the round had come past me, but later we figured that a round had hit a log over the trench and ricocheted down into the trooper's lung.) I took the wounded trooper's M-16 rifle and handed him my cocked 45-cal. pistol. Big Mistake! As he rotated left and collapsed in pain, he squeezed off three rounds into the side of the trench. It would have been me except for his twisting motion as he sunk down.

11

Had the trench been straighter, we would have perished there. At one point still unconvinced that we were under hostile fire, I yelled out, "Cease fire, we're Marines." I had a thought that the ARVN mistakenly fired on us. I didn't understand the Vietnamese answer I received but the tone of the enemy soldier's voice removed all doubt but that we were destined for annihilation. We never saw anyone to shoot at and within seconds, troops from our perimeter came out to our rescue. We found a place to scoot out from the trench and retire to our perimeter. Meanwhile, an airborne Forward Observer (FO) who watched the whole thing from his small plane was bringing in artillery fire to disrupt the ambush and drive off the enemy. I know now that they were the four, ARVN-

12

looking troops we had seen earlier.  As the ambushers departed, they scarfed up the mailbag and all the C-rats boxes they could carry.

Were they regular ARVN soldiers that played both sides against the middle?  Were they VC wearing captured clothing and equipment to deceive the enemy?  Either way, it wasn't pleasant to think about.

Our biggest success from our raid on Go Noi Island was the discovery of a mine factory which was being serviced by the young women that did laundry and ran small stores around our Battalion HQ in Phong Loc.  These girls were keeping tabs on us for the VC and running mines up Highway 1 on their bikes.  What a mess we were in Vietnam.  These same sixteen-year old girls that sell Cokes by the roadside had been trying all the time to blow us up. The feeling of betrayal from this experience permeated the morale of every one of us. We had worked hard to gain respect and show friendship toward the civilian population around our Battalion CP only to find that our friends were, in actuality, our enemies.

I took the absolute worst ass chewing of my life from Captain Tom Pratt for getting ambushed, getting ambushed and having wounded, getting ambushed and losing the US Mail, for getting ambushed without a radio and for going anywhere without a radio. Oh, did I mention losing the mail? We all had to write our loved ones, admit this humiliating experience and urge them not to open any strange packages. So, ends my recollection of the 1967 Echo Company raid on Go Noi Island.

Later in life when I deserved a tongue lashing for my behavior, I would always think to myself, "Well, you're good but you're no Tom Pratt."

Echo 2/1 67-68 - Captain Tom Pratt

*I served under many fine officers, but I must tell you that Tom Pratt was*

*one of the finest Marines I've ever*
*known.*

After sharing this Internet message with various 2/1 veterans, I received this account on the 18th of May 1999, thirty-two years after the facts from former Marine Don Hollan then in Cincinnati Ohio.

Hello
Lee.............................................
.............................................

I remember the adventure of Go Noi island as if it were yesterday. Maybe this will help you remember Terry Feninga. Terry always carried a grease gun (Thompson 45-auto machinegun) not an M-16. The night of the river crossing Terry & I were walking tail-end-Charlie & became separated from the rest of the platoon and we were at the rear of the Company. Terry was in front of me, so I was the last man Terry usually just ditty-bopped or lolly gagged & we got behind. I remembered when I had last seen someone & had a good idea of where we were going so I took the point, we caught up to you all at the river just in time for us to cross. After crossing I took the tail again. (You couldn't leave Terry alone; hard telling where you would find him.) After the crossing, we settled in for the night. I stood the first 2 watches. Terry was beat and I was still keyed up from him getting us separated. I woke Robby Roberts up to stand the last watch, I finally got a little sleep, it was right at dawn, not good day light yet when I woke to see a VC reaching for my M-16. I jumped up and got it, he took off running & I opened up on him about the same time everyone saw him and opened up.  We got him.  Robby got a huge lump on the side of his head from the butt of my 16.  At that time, I really wanted to shoot him, but it passed.

I remember going with you to the company CP, stopping when we saw the ARVNs and asking you if there was supposed to be any friendlies in the area. I will always remember that ambush, the Marine behind you that got shot had a sucking chest wound, the first one of many that I saw while over there.
   Without any hesitation the rest of the platoon came to our aid.  I really wanted those C-rats.  Terry had forgotten his (again) so I shared mine with him.  We had been out since the day the river crossing. That was just another

day that I was proud to be a member of Echo Company, Second Battalion 1st Marines, 3rd herd as Archie always said.

Thanks for the memories...As always........Don


## Terry Feninga

Thank you, Don Hollan for asking me if I remember Terry Feninga. Yes, I do. Terry was thirty-two years old, half again as old as any of us boys. He spoke slowly and deeply and was not anywhere near the fastest boat in the fleet. Some called him the "old man" because of his age.

He was a biker and he owned a Harley. He also owned and loved a "grease gun" which is a 45 caliber

19

sub-machine gun. The grease gun is not to be confused with the beautifully sculpted 45 caliber, Thompson sub-machine gun that G-men like Elliott Ness carried on The Untouchables. No, the grease gun looked more like.........well, a grease gun. Before he joined the Marines, Terry would mount his grease gun to the handlebars of his Harley and ride down some deserted country road shooting at beer cans. I can just imagine what kind of marksmanship he experienced with this crude and inaccurate relic.

When Terry shipped out for Vietnam, he disassembled his beloved grease gun and taped it to his legs with electrical tape. Consequently, he carried his beloved grease gun on patrols instead of his issued weapon. We all learned to hate it when he would open up in the middle of the night at some dark shadow he thought had moved. He never killed anything, but he sure did wake up the countryside.

I remember once when we changed our position after nightfall. This was a common practice in the Phung Ngu area because it reduced the likelihood of night attack if we could set up under darkness. The rear guard heard noises from the position we had just vacated. There was gunfire. We stopped to figure out what was happening. Turns out Terry had the radio, so he told us that he had just been fired on. I asked if he was alone. He said, "yup." I said for him to just be quiet and not to shoot and that we'd send someone back to fetch him.

Terry was killed on Operation Medina. In my story on Medina, Terry was the wounded Marine in the intersection of the trails. He took three rounds in his chest, was unconscious and bleeding badly. After the enemy threat was reduced, we called a medivac. Our Corpsman stayed with Terry giving him mouth to mouth and CPR. We learned by radio that Terry was pronounced dead after takeoff.

In 1908, Lord Baden-Powell, a retired British General, wrote the Scouting Handbook for Boys which initiated the worldwide Boy Scout movement. I was a scout, an Eagle Scout, and I loved the handbook which told how to mark a trail, treat poison ivy, set an animal trap, and thousands of other interesting scouting things. When I joined the Marines, they gave me the Guidebook for

Marines. I still have it and will forever. It tells about chemical warfare, cold weather indoctrination, small arms, grenades, flame-throwers and thousands of other interesting Marine Corps things.

What follows, dear reader, is my version of a handbook. It is a compilation of short quips, disconnected memories, and amusing antidotes that don't fit the chronological stories I've tried to tell elsewhere. So here and there, I've included information I call Handbook information.

Vietnam Combat Handbook
VC Security Alarms

The Viet Cong were ingenious guerrilla fighters who were adept at developing simple homegrown devices and techniques to thwart the might and technology of the US war machine.  The VC Security Alarm was an excellent example of that ingenuity.  At nightfall, VC who took refuge in a village, or simply returned home, would set out alarms to keep from being surprised by Marine night patrols.

The alarm is built with a tin can. Two bamboo splints are lashed to its sides with rubber bands or string.  One splint is longer than the other, so that it can be pushed into the soft rice paddy mud to hold the device about 12 to 18 inches above the ground.  The two splints extend above the can top, actually the can bottom now facing skyward.  A washer or a flattened bottle cap with a hole in it is suspended between the two upright splints by rubber bands so that it can be twisted up like a propeller on a toy airplane.  Now a small stick is placed through the hole in the washer to keep it from spinning.  A string tied to the stick is pulled across a trail and tied off in the brush. Now when an intruder hits the string in the darkness, the stick comes out of the washer and the washer spins striking the tin can with a loud metallic chatter. It's like a fire alarm bell in the middle of the night when maximum stealth is being applied. The chatter of one of these alarms will flatten a Marine patrol and bring their hearts into their throats.  The beauty of these alarms is that they can be taken up before dawn, hidden and no one is the wiser.

Vietnam Combat Handbook
VC Temporary Booby Traps

Whenever a US grenade fell into VC hands, it usually ended up as a temporary bobby trap.  It was used in the same way as the night alarms. The grenade was secured to a bamboo splint with string or rubber bands. The grenade pin was replaced with a safety pin (as in baby diaper verity). After nightfall, the grenade could be set with a string across a trail and the safety pin unclasped. So now, the sleeping VC would hear a BLAM! ........... instead of a clatter. Hopefully, the VC would also achieve a few US casualties in the process. The safety pin arrangement facilitated the retrieval of the booby trap before dawn. Re-clasping the safety pin rendered the grenade safe until it was used again.

I was wounded three times in Vietnam. (Not unusual, everyone in a rifle company was either killed or wounded except one extremely lucky individual who did an amazing eighteen months without a scratch.) I've told about being wounded twice elsewhere. The first time I was wounded was in the Phung Ngu area. It was night and we were trying to gain a position of advantage before dawn.

BLAM! That's all the warning you get. A small metal fragment hit me on the last rib on my left. I still see it on my X-rays. Grenades are funny. The M26A1 has an effective casualty radius of fifteen meters but the killing radius is quite a bit smaller. The grenade had a smooth thin metal cover and is designed to throw shrapnel that comes from a coil of serrated wire. The theory is that the serrated wire will break up more consistently in a regular spherical pattern. Older grenades like the cast iron pineapple looking grenade of WW II, the MK2, would break up in irregular patterns.  So, the piece of wire about the size of a broken pencil lead hit me giving me a pinprick and a minor thud on my rib.  I was far enough away from the blast that it was not a serious wound.

**Vietnam Combat Handbook**
**Hazing**

The Battalion perimeter in Phong Loc was really quite comfortable. We had an officer's club, an NCO club and a club for enlisted men. We also had firing ranges, showers, and plywood barracks with cots.

*Shower and Mule.*

Not long after arriving, I was asked if I had seen Sergeant Gonzalez' monkey. Of course, I had not and was quite curious about the whole thing.

They took me over to the Golf Company area where I met Gunnery Sergeant Gonzalez. He and his beer-guzzling pals were lounging around in the shade behind some barracks. The affable Gonzalez was the epitome of the Marine Corps lifer NCO. He was short, a little pudgy, heavily tattooed and he sported a beautiful oversized handlebar moustache. Gonzalez wore his 45-cal. pistol in a shoulder holster, puffed on a cheroot and he was nothing if he wasn't colorful.

The monkey was named Chi-chi. He was on a twenty-foot leash and had a tall bamboo tree to climb on. Sergeant Gonzalez coaxed Chi-chi down from his perch and introduced me to him in the gentlest terms. I know now that the hypnotic cajoling was for me; not Chi-chi, because as soon as Chi-chi climbed up my leg and back to sit upon my shoulder he bit me on the ear. I flinched, the monkey scampered up the bamboo tree screeching like a banshee and Sergeant Gonzalez and his beer-guzzling pals exploded in riotous laughter. It was the greatest sport to be had in the whole country no doubt. Simple men amuse themselves in simple ways.

Vietnam Combat Handbook
Vietnamese Graves

Sleeping on graves deserves some explanation. The Vietnamese peasants work the land for a living. The land is everything. Ancestor worship is also part of their culture. Therefore, they bury their dead vertically in the rice paddy so as to require as little crop yielding land as possible, leaving a grave mound above the water in the paddy for multiple burials (6-8). Grave mounds were usually covered in thick grass and offered good cover. These graves were here and there but most often in clusters. When we slept on patrol, one man out of four stood his turn at watch.

Vietnam Combat Handbook
Hammer and Anvil

This is military terminology for a pincer movement by two units where one is stationary (the anvil) and one is mobile (the hammer). Echo Company, Third Platoon was assigned as an anvil for a Company that was moving from our south. It was in the Phung Ngu area, actually on the southern boarder marked by a river with deep banks.

Rivers are dangerous. Boarder areas are dangerous. They are like the dividing lines between police jurisdictions. Sooner or later the bad guys get the picture that the area isn't patrolled as often as other areas. The river with its steep banks provides cover. We set up and waited for the better part of an afternoon. We felt that the dangerous part of the mission was just getting there and getting back, and we never really expected to see any action. But then, the third squad, about 300 meters to my left, called on the radio to say that there were about twenty VC to their front. They asked for orders. I said, "shoot 'em!" They blasted away for a while scattering the VC. Neither the second nor the first squad saw anything. We were too spread out. It was dusk and time to pull out. Did we kill? I don't know.

## Vietnam Combat Handbook
## Early Morning Ambush

Phung Ngu area. We had obtained our position under cover of darkness and we were undiscovered. Dawn came. A trooper told me that three-armed VC were crossing our front in the shoulder-high rice. There were only eight of us there at the time. I went to the M-60 machine gun. When the time was right, I signaled for them to open up. Click! The gun jammed. There was only a rifleman and a 3.5-inch rocket team. The rifle would have been a waste of a good ambush. The rocket team was loaded with a White Phosphorous round. They begged me for permission to shoot.

White Phosphorous is a chemical that burns when exposed to the air.  The shell explodes in a 35-meter bursting radius.  Unfortunately, it leaves an enormously heavy cloud of white smoke that takes forever to clear.  I knew if we fired the rocket that would be the end of the ambush.  Firing the rifle would be the same.  Maybe we would hit one but the others would duck under the rice and run out of the killing zone.

I gave the rocket man the nod and he put the round exactly where they were.  Blam!  White smoke.  We waited.  When we entered the killing zone to check for damage, there was nothing, not a sign, not a clue.  Did we kill?  I don't know.

## Vietnam Combat Handbook
## Road Side Refreshment

You could buy a Coca-Cola sometimes on ice if you were on Route 1............. not soda, not grape, not Pepsi, not any other brand but Coca-Cola. There were always a few entrepreneurs, usually old women with Coca-Cola and sometimes ice. Occasionally, we found small loaves of bread to buy. If there was a roach in your bread, you just pinched it out and continued eating. Such was the state of affairs.

MAR 1968

*Convenient Stop'N Go along Rte 1.*

## Quang Tri

Quang Tri is the capital city of the northern province of I-Corps. When we arrived in the Quang Tri area, we set up a Battalion Perimeter in some low rolling hills and pitched tents. The ground was rocky and difficult to dig in. So, most of our operation was above ground.

We were running patrols out of this place, sometimes for a day to three days. The troops like to give the heavy squad radio to the new men that come into country. It's all part of the hazing process. One new trooper had become so involved with the radio that he inadvertently left his rifle in the field following a break. The squad leader came to me at dusk after we had returned to the Battalion perimeter. He said that he didn't know quite how to break the news but that a new Private had left his weapon in a village hooch at the last break. Without a moment's thought, I took the Private, the squad leader and one other in a Mighty Mite and we burst forth like gangbusters into the countryside in pursuit of the missing weapon.

The Mighty Mite was a jeep-like product by American Motors but smaller. I doubt if a Mighty Mite could achieve a speed of 35 mph. Originally designed to be dropped 15 feet from a moving helicopter, the Mighty Might had been a miserable failure for its original mission but evidently good enough for our Marine Corps.

*Me with others and the Mighty Mite.*

Leaving the perimeter that late in the day in haste was near suicidal. We could all have been killed and never heard from again. I wasn't concerned about that. I was concerned about what I would have to say to my Company Commander if we came back without the rifle.

We wheeled into the village and found the place the Private remembered. We began flashing piasters (Vietnamese money) and Military Payment Certificates (MPC) and jabbering like crazy men for a rifle. Finally, one old gentleman understood. He reached up into the grass roof of his hooch and withdrew an M-16 rifle. We gave him the money, thanked him profusely ("Come on am") and got the hell out of there.

That evening when things were back to normal, the squad leader came to me to thank me. He also wanted me to know that the serial number on the rifle was not the same as on the rifle lost by the Private. I told him that all was well that ended well and this would just have to be our little secret.

## Vietnam Combat Handbook
## C-Rations

They came packaged in boxes of twelve Meals, Individual Rations. Now, a reasonable person with a command of the language would simply say twelve individual meals. But, military language will not conform to reason.

I don't remember the combinations now, but each meal had a number, like B-3. Eventually, you'd learn which meals you could tolerate and which you'd rather do without. Don't get me wrong, the food packed in C-Ration cans was not bad tasting food, it's just that if you have only twelve choices for your food for months at a time, you grow tired of the selection.

I survived C-Rations by having my family mail me ketchup. You can eat anything with enough ketchup. I used to make a casserole using one of the large cans. I cut a layer of bread which came in its own can, spoon in some ham and eggs, a squeeze of ketchup and then repeat the process filling the can. The casserole cooks in 5-8 seconds with a golf-ball size portion of C-4 plastic explosive. Don't worry, it can't explode without a blasting cap but it burns with such sputtering intensity you'll think that the can will melt.

One of the meals comes with a small tin of peanut butter. If you squirt mosquito repellant on its surface to light it, the peanut butter will burn making a nice flambeau. I never had to use it but could have in order to mark landing zones in the dark.

Packed in every case of C-rats were several P-38's. That's what we called them although I've heard many other nicknames for these small folding can openers. I still carry one on my key chain. It makes a good screwdriver, fingernail cleaner, box opener and occasionally I open a can with it.

So now let me tell you about K-Rations. Unlike C-Rations, which is food packed in cans, ham and Lima beans, cheese and crackers, chocolate, etc., K-rations are a modern field food of the type that you would find in a hiking store. It is dehydrated stuff in a plastic pouch. You just add water, stir and poof your chicken tetrazzini comes to life. K-rations was food to die for and we had none. On the other hand, Army troops were well supplied with all kinds of nice foodstuffs and equipment. They had so much, and we had so little. It only made since that when we came into contact with Army troops that we should enrich ourselves from the largess of the US taxpayer. And, there were many a dark night when Marines performed the midnight requisition while the Army slept.

## Vietnam Combat Handbook
## Side Arms

Ever since being ambushed on Go Noi Island and being armed only with a pistol, I sought and eventually obtained a bigger weapon. The Marines did not want their field officers caring rifles. In the heat of battle, the officer is supposed to be engaged in all manner of leadership and communication roles and does not have time to fire upon the enemy. Consequently, officers are supposed to carry only their side arm for personal protection. Nevertheless, the "pop-gun" feeling had never left me and if I couldn't carry a rifle, then I wanted something with some oomph. Finally, I was allowed to draw a pump-action, twelve-gauge shotgun from an armory. It held about eight to ten rounds and had what I considered to be substantial stopping power.

Once we were on some mountaintop we had climbed from a stream below. Just a few of us ventured into the thick undergrowth leaving the others to rest at the summit. We were several hundred meters from the main body reconnoitering the area when we heard noises. It sounded like a patrol of men working their way through the brush. Their path was going to cross ours about ten to fifteen meters away. Leaves and branches were rustling. Twigs were snapping.

We couldn't see a thing. We were very still. Could these be our own men? We waited. If we shouted, would they fire back? Why not just give them some double ought buckshot from the trench gun? But then, I'd have to rack it; too much noise. Let's wait until we know for sure. Whatever it was crossed our path without noticing us or being recognized and descended the ridge to our left.

I radioed an airborne forward observer to discuss the possibility of naval gunfire. This was the only kind of artillery support that could reach us. The FO heard me out and suggested that we may have happened on a rock ape. Yes, of course, it was some type of wildlife. Maybe even a rock ape.

I never fired the shotgun except on the firing range.

Operation Medina

The adventures of Third Platoon, Echo Company, 2nd Battalion, First Marines, Republic of Vietnam 1967.

Operation Medina was a Battalion sized, search and destroy mission in the Hai Lang Forest. There was a lot of fighting during Medina, most of which Echo was not involved in. I'm told that Hotel Company was ambushed badly as the operation was coming to a close and that many casualties were taken. The place was a jungle. We usually worked with 1:25000 photo-picto maps with contour lines every 10 meters. With such maps, you could easily identify your spot on the ground using roads, tree lines, elevation, rivers, etc. The maps were very accurate, and you could call in artillery fire with confidence. When we moved into the Hai Lang Forest, we changed to a 1:50000 (details four times smaller) with a contour elevation every 20 meters. That's sixty feet, my friends, and that's not very helpful at all. There were no roads, villages, etc., in the jungle. The map was solid green. The only thing we had to go on was the contour lines, which were too far apart to be able to read the map with the limited visibility in the jungle. As a consequence, we stayed lost. Once, the Battalion Commander called in helicopters and fired starburst clusters through the canopy so that we could be located by air.

This operation lasted a week or more. As usual, Echo was in the lead with my platoon, third platoon, on point. We had two guys that were natural born Indian fighters, Corporal Tilo Oesterreich and Lance Corporal Dennis Knoblock. In the jungle, there were two very dangerous places to be. One was on a bald mountaintop. From a bald, you could be seen for miles and be fired upon with rockets, mortars or artillery. The second dangerous place was in the deep ravines where water ran. These mountain streams were what the enemy used. They didn't have helicopters to bring water to the top, so it was likely that their base camps were down low.

Tilo Rudolf Oesterreich – Echo Co 2/1
KIA 7 April 1968 – Panel 48E Row 45

We came upon a stream. We all got cautions. Suddenly, there was machine gun fire and return fire. I ran forward with others to find that Tilo and Knobby had stumbled onto an NVA hospital complex guarded by a single rear guard with a machine gun. They took him out in a few short minutes. You think it easy? Go ahead. Take a machine gun away from a determined enemy soldier. Thank God, we had no casualties. These empty hospitals were about 60 feet long, open air buildings with grass roofs and wooden floors. There were other living quarters and supply buildings. Echo Company followed us into this clearing and long after we left we could hear the crackle as the flames consumed this jungle facility.

We were in the jungle for many days with no resupply. We were hungry. We had taken a sleeve of rice from the hospital complex. It was like a pant leg, filled with rice, tied off at each end with a rope that could be slung over the neck and shoulder. The rice was crude, unprocessed nodules of grain. If you know Uncle Ben's, you wouldn't recognize this material as rice. With a little C-4 or a heat tab, you could boil up a small hand full which gave quite a satisfying result.

Later, we came upon another clearing. The canopy was whole, but the underbrush was cut out. This place looked like a Boy Scout campground. There were worn places on the ground where hundreds of men had recently slept. We were moving cautiously but rapidly. I didn't want to be caught in the middle of the clearing and I wanted to get to the other side quickly. I was about three fourths across when a machine gun barked to my left. I ran to my left, toward a little stream and a trail that went away from the clearing, backward and to the left. It intersected with another trail that left the clearing at 90 degrees to the left. So, there was a little triangle of brush formed by the two trails and the stream between the men on the short trail and the clearing where the main body was.

When I got to the men, there were three on the short trail and one dying (Terry Feninga) in the intersection of the two trails. More machine-gun fire. We mistakenly thought the fire was coming from the right. Then, a grenade sound, like a rock falling through the trees. Being close enough to throw grenades was not good news particularly when we did not know where the enemy was. The grenade landed in the triangle of brush not far from us. I was sitting down almost shoulder to shoulder with the others facing the grenade. I tried to lean backward into the brush, but it was not forgiving. So, I pulled my helmet over my face before the grenade went off. We were sprayed with shrapnel. A nickel-sized piece of shrapnel hit me on my third rib on the right side. My flak jacket was open. It cut a hole in my shirt and left a bloody spot but did not penetrate. I felt that we were all dead men if we didn't find that machine gunner quickly.

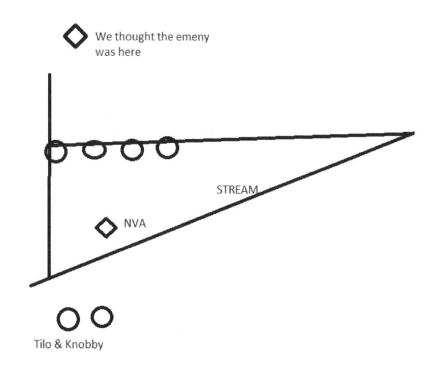

We thought the emeny was here

STREAM

NVA

Tilo & Knobby

Meanwhile, Tilo was in the main clearing. He had figured out that the machine gunner was in a hole in the triangle of brush. Those of us on the trail had it completely wrong. We had no idea that the bad guy was so close, practically right in front of us. Since the bad guy was between the main body and us, none of us could have fired without hitting friendlies. Tilo crawled into the thicket and located the enemy only after touching the top of his head. Tilo dispatched him immediately I was told, and we were saved.

Tilo and his family were refugees from East Germany. He was later killed by friendly mortar fire. Our Captain was registering 81 mm mortars around our position before setting up the company. Four shells came in on top of Tilo's fire team. Three died instantly including Tilo. Every man of ours was a comrade whether he was personally known as a friend or just another brother in uniform. When a brother fell, it was a time for remorse. If the brother was a dear friend, all the more reason for anguish and bereavement. But I tell you, dear reader, there were not losses more bitterly suffered than the loss of those dear friends and comrades that fell to friendly fire. All too frequently, and because of the lethal nature of all tools in combat, men died from the killing power of our own weapons misdirected by accident or used too close to our forces.

I wrote Tilo up for a Silver Star but was later wounded in Quang Tri and evacuated. Tilo's medal was never approved. After I got out of the Corps, I got correspondence from USMC about the event. Knobby had asked his Senator to look into the matter. I wrote him up again. Several years later, I wrote to Tilo's sister who said Tilo never got his medal. When I was forty-two years old, exactly twice as old as I was in Vietnam, the traveling Vietnam Memorial Wall was in Houston on Memorial Day. I

took all my correspondence on Tilo
and my Bronze Star and I
presented them to Tilo beneath his
name on the wall. It was not big
thing except it made me feel a little
better to know that even though
the US government would not give
Tilo a medal, I could give him a
medal and I did. He was a
courageous warrior; a fine young
man and he made a significant
contribution to our country. He
saved my life and I will never forget
him.

##### ----- AUGUST 27, 2012 -----

I've just returned from an Echo Raiders reunion in Prescott Valley Arizona. The Internet is a wonderful thing. I went to Prescott Valley to see Captain Tom Pratt and Dennis "Knobby" Knoblock. I have learned so much and wish to make corrections to the above story that I believed until now was true. The others that died with Tilo on April 7, 1968 were LCpl John Mount of Vineland, New Jersey, and PFC Thomas Nash of Atlanta, Georgia. Knobby was not there that day as he had been previously wounded and evacuated. Tilo had extended his tour of duty.

At a quiet lake, Lynx Lake, after a splendid boat ride and a filling lunch, we talked of many things. Naturally, we began to reminisce.

At some point, Knobby recounted an episode wherein he killed an NVA soldier who was armed with a machine gun in some brush. My heart raced. I checked what he remembered with what I remembered, and it became clear to me at last. It was not Tilo who crawled through the brush to save me and the others who were pinned down on the short trail by the stream. It was Knobby. When the shooting began, it was Tilo who recognized the danger we were in. Tilo requested permission to lead his fire team into the brush. At his side, Knobby saw black hair just over some brush and took aim. He questioned whether it was a Marine or an enemy. He did not want to kill one of us, but he recognized that either way, people were going to die if he did not act. He took aim and fired.

Tilo is certainly also responsible for saving me.  But, at last I was able to throw my arms around the neck of the brave Marine whose courage and aim actually did the deed.  These two fellows are my heroes.  I owe them my life as do the others who were pinned down on that short trail by the little stream in the jungle.

The Internet and military reunions have helped me with facts.  So many times, I discovered what I had believed to be true was not absolutely true or not true at all.  There is a reason for this.  While you might expect that after an engagement with the enemy there was a lengthy debriefing wherein all the testimony is taken, the facts are laid straight, and the chronology is settled.  In my experience, this never happened.

There isn't any time nor safety for conducting an inquiry. Our mission was always to close with and destroy the enemy before he did the same to us. Consequently, what any Marine or soldier knew about an engagement was what he saw and experienced. The rest was hearsay, sometimes hearsay passed through multiple mouths.

## Fire in the Grass

Once, Echo Company was in a place of tall grass. Tall grass is everywhere in the backcountry of Vietnam. This place was rolling, small hills with only an occasional sparsely populated tree lines and no civilian population. Of course, registering artillery and mortar points around your perimeter was textbook training for combat officers.  But, experience taught that there were consequences. Need I remind you of the tragic death of the three Marines including Tilo Oesterreich?  The idea is to pick out some strategic spots around your position, have the mortars or artillery fire upon these targets and then register the coordinates.  Registration is the term used by the Fire Direction Center (FDC) which has calculated the correct direction, angle and charge for the shells to reach the specific targets.  This information is saved for future use.  If during the night your position is attacked, fire can quickly be brought or adjusted from these spots.

It's good textbook tactics.  Trouble is that it causes more trouble than its worth.  If you have acquired your position without being discovered by the enemy, registration will surely call attention to your presence. Then there is always the possibility that a short round or a Fire Direction Control Center (FDC) error (as in the case of the above-mentioned tragedy) will endanger your own. Now comes the next bad thing to result from registration. The first white phosphorus round which came into the tall grass set the grass afire. Imagine if you will, a wall of fire spreading out toward your position from the flaming dry grass standing eight to eleven feet tall. It was a mad dash without orders and without organization. It was every man for himself as we picked up our belongings and chose the best path to evade the worst of the fire.

During the scramble a small, blinded deer came into my path. No bigger than a medium-sized dog, he was burned on his hindquarters and other places on his legs. I captured it with little trouble, tied it to my belt and had some idea of an eventual feast. But, the deer was too heavy, and feasting was not something that we had time or security to do. I let the critter go; knowing that it would soon die for it had not capacity to survive its burns and blindness.

## Wounded

My last day as a Platoon Commander occurred in Quang Tri province under Captain Baker. We had been on a Company sized sweep for several days and were making our way back to the Battalion perimeter. It was getting toward dusk and we were trying to find a place to set in the Company for the night. Third Platoon was on point as usual and there had been no contact during the entire patrol.

We passed a bombed-out Catholic Cathedral. I'm told it is called the Notre Dame de La Vang and it is pictured in the New York Times, August 16, 1998. The place was surreal. The Cathedral sat on a hill; no others for miles and there were pine trees around; none others in the country as far as I know. The Cathedral itself was haunting and out of place. Nothing else was around but typical agricultural countryside; rice paddies, bamboo tree lines and villages.

To our right was a big irrigation ditch. You would call it a bayou in Texas. I had to have a look into the ditch. It was the perfect place for the enemy to approach us with protection for escape. As the point squad passed a small trail over a culvert to our right, without thinking, I peeled off right to cross the culvert and head over about 20 meters to the right to look into the ditch. My radioman and one other rifleman instinctively followed me. Blam!

The mine, a Z-10 grenade sized with a pull friction fuse, was hidden under the culvert. The brick culvert, no doubt, absorbed most of the blast and probably saved my leg and foot. As it was, only the worst of the shrapnel escaped the brick to wound the three of us. My error in crossing this culvert was a classic boo-boo. Had I seen a trooper of mine attempting to do the same thing, I would have stopped him. We were in mine country and our Battalion had already suffered enormous casualties. This was a trail and trails are terrible for mines. Worse, this was a narrow place in the trail. The wet places to either side of the culvert channeled the victim across the mine. Finally, this culvert was a wonderful place to hide explosives.

First, I smelled the black powder, then I heard the sound, and finally I saw the flash of light. It was all backward and all in slow motion. I tried to run but my feet weren't working. When I hit the ground, I searched for my weapon thinking that we would be attacked instantly. We weren't. The two behind me seemed to be hurt worse than I was. I did some cussing for making such a stupid mistake. Others were taking charge, binding our wounds and calling in a medivac chopper.

As the chopper took off with us, the VC opened up on it. They were very close, and they were in great numbers. I feared being shot in the back with no place to hide. Others that came in wounded to the Battalion Aide Station (BAS) told us that there was much fighting that night. The BAS in Quang Tri was a tent, just like you see on MASH.

The doctor in the BAS (Dr. Lee) was amused by my case. I took small wounds in my right forearm and right buttocks. I had much greater wounds in my left and right ankles. What amused him was the wound in my right ankle just above the boot line. Marines don't tuck their trousers into their boots. They use a blousing band, a spring or elastic around the leg. The trousers are folded up and under. This method keeps out leeches, ticks and other critters.  My choice was to use a metal spring.  The shrapnel had driven the spring into my flesh and was now dangling out of my wound like TV rabbit ears.

Of course, there was an audience. "Hey, come get a load of this."  The Doctor called for his camera, and then when ready for surgery, he called for the wire cutters from his tool chest.  I think I had local anesthetic only because I was not out for the surgery.  The doctor only removed visible shrapnel and did not do damage fishing around. He merely cleaned the wounds and sewed them up.  There was enough meat and skin missing from my right leg that sewing up was like stringing a banjo.

I was sore beyond description. The next day, a chopper carried me to Cam Ranh Bay, which is an enormous US military complex and hospital area in the south of the country on the coast.   I started walking in four weeks with occasional strolls on the beach. The uneven ground helped me to regain my strength.  I recuperated there for a total of six-weeks and then I rejoined Echo Company at Con Thien as Executive Officer.

## Con Thien, The Place of Angles

This place consisted of three gently rising and interlocking hilltops overlooking the Song (river) Bien Hai, about 12 kilometers away.  The Song Bien Hai divides South from North Vietnam.  Con Thien was in the middle of Robert MacNamarra's Demilitarized Zone (DMZ) and was a prominent terrain feature about midway from the South China Sea coast and Laos. In the Vietnamese language, Con Thien translates to the "place of angles."

*Echo 2/1 67-68 - Prayer at Con Thien*

*Yes, we went to church, at least this once that I recall.*

I came by vehicle over what was a river of mud. Large crushed stone had been laid over the road to try to create a passable roadway. The stones sank quickly and had to be replaced. Inside the perimeter, there was an Amphibious Tractor three quarters buried off the roadway. As time went along, the Am Track sank and eventually disappeared beneath the sticky goo of Con Thien during the monsoon.

At Con Thien, there were tremendous living bunkers sunk into the ground by bulldozer and made of heavy timbers. We called them Di Marker Bunkers. These were covered with massive mounds of dirt and sand bags. Other fighting and living bunkers were located closer to the wire. Although, I must say that everything was located close to the wire at Con Thien. The position of the base left it subject to enemy tank fire, recoilless rifle fire, mortar fire and the relentless artillery fire.

The NVA used 152 mm shells, as big as any we used. The biggest gun the US had in Vietnam was the 155 mm howitzer. (As I later learned, the US had and used 175 mm howitzers in Vietnam.) When a barrage of 152's came in, you know you have been shelled. There is a boom, boom, boom way off in the distance, then about four seconds later a whistling zip and deafening crash. A 152 mm shell can explode through eight feet of dirt and break open a Di Marker Bunker with sides of 2X6 lumber. See a repair of a direct hit in this photo.

The Marines in this bunker were spared because of a wall of C-Rations that partitioned the bunker.

Once our ammunition pit was hit. Mortars, shells, flares and bullets exploded for twenty-four hours. The fire would die down and then start popping again. My photograph of the aftermath shows spent and burned ammunition of all kinds scattered over the ground of Con Thien for about 300 meters in all directions. I'm sure that cost the taxpayers several million dollars.

We spent Christmas of 1967 at Con Thien. A truck convoy bought us hot food. It was a glorious hiatus from the tedium of C-rations.

Echo 2/1 67-68 - Christmas 1967

*Yippee! Christmas dinner.*

We were there for the Vietnamese holiday of Tet (Vietnamese New

Year), January 1968.  Weeks before our Battalion CO was asking for a "gung-ho" lieutenant to lead some volunteers into North Vietnam and "snatch" an emery soldier and bring him back alive.  I politely said "No" when I was asked.  This group of six was practicing their craft out east of Con Thien when a superior enemy force pinned them down.  What they observed was thousands of NVA regulars, trucks and tanks streaming by and heading south toward Hue. Meanwhile back at Con Thien, we were amazed to hear hundreds of artillery pieces firing.  This time the shells did not land on us but cut through the air over our heads for southern targets.  The Tet offensive had begun.  This time Con Thien was out of the fighting. No one came for us.  But, in the rest of the country, a war was blazing.

Our company first sergeant, Gunnery Sergeant Weathers was killed by artillery. Weathers was a decent man many of us regarded as a father figure. He and Captain Quinlan were running for a bunker. A shell struck the corner of the bunker they were running for. Weathers body was blown back into Captain Quinlan who was bruised from head to toe and with ruptured eardrums.

*Unfortunately, the only photo I have of Captain Quinlan is beside the latrine.*

All of a sudden, I was acting Company Commander. We were on a Company size patrol to the west of Con Thien. Suddenly, a CH-46 helicopter landed in our midst. I looked into the back to see that the cargo area was full of beer cases. I went to the front and took the telephone handset by the co-pilots seat. He said, "Where is Con Thien?" I held up my map to the glass, showed him our position and the location of Con Thien, then I pointed real big towards the base so he and the pilot could get the idea. I can't remember what happened before or after this unusual event. Funny what you remember. No telling what you forget.

Corporal Melendez, squad leader, was a natural born leader and a hell of a nice person. He and others had been guarding truck convoys which we sent south every morning to fetch sandbags which were filled by Vietnamese laborers at some southern point. On the way home one evening, he was on the last truck with three others of his squad. When they loaded the truck, they sort of built a fort of sandbags.  Then they laid down for a nap.  Their truck was hit by an RPG-7 rocket, which knocked off a front wheel, sending the truck into a ditch.  Four NVA soldiers got up blasting away, closing in to finish off the driver.  It was the last day of their lives.  Melendez and crew popped up out of the sandbags and returned the favor.

Echo 2/1 67-68 - Corporal Melendez

*Melendez was eating his C-rats.*
*Picture taken somewhere in the*
*Phung Nu area, 1967.*

Another time, Melendez was setting in night listening posts to the west of Con Thien. One of his men, he thought, the radio operator had left his post and was squatting in the open moonlight. Melendez went over, squatted in front of the man's face and proceeded to whisper "a piece of his mind" when he suddenly realized that the radio operator was not his but theirs. The two reached this conclusion at the same time. So, Melendez just slugged the guy and ran off. Melendez lay low throughout the night as enemy troops poked and probed through the bushes looking for him. Melendez was lovable and lucky.

We used a diesel-powered mule to move food, water and ammunition. It was a two/four-wheel drive/steer platform about three feet wide and five feet long. The men would fill five-gallon Jerry cans from a water buffalo and mule them over to an outdoor shower. It took three men and a ladder to pass the Jerry cans of water to the 55-gallon drum, at the top of the shower.

Many years after Vietnam, I got a surprise telephone call from my old radio operator. He looked me up because he needed a character reference for a judge; something to do with an arrest of some kind. Anyway, he asked me if I had seen the book. "What book", I asked. So, he sent me the book, Of Guts and Glory, by Combat Correspondents of the United States Marine Corps, Edited by Jack Lewis, published by

Challenge Publications, Incorporated, 7805 Deering Avenue, Canoga Park, California 91304. September 1968. The book is a compilation of stories from the Sea Tiger, a Vietnam era Navy/Marine newspaper.

The passage he referenced reads:

Then there is the story of three Marines, who barely escaped an enemy barrage. For four days, the enemy had been dropping in a few artillery rounds only in the early morning and late evening. Considering the record, the three men of the First Marine regiment headed for the shower stall near the end of their compound, expecting to get clean before the action started.

"I had just finished my shower and was drying off," says Second Lieutenant Lee Suydam of Montgomery, Alabama, a twenty-one-year-old company commander. "I had just said something to the others as to how embarrassing it would be to have a couple of rounds drop in now. That was when we heard that screaming whistle of incoming."

Suydam, Sergeant Peter G. Walsh of Hamilton, Ontario, and Corporal John Mac Donnell of Patterson, New Jersey, burst from the showers, still damp, and made for the cover of a rocky outcropping as the first rounds exploded nearby.

"For just a second, we debated putting on our clothes or just to put on our helmets and flak jackets and run," Walsh reports. "When the next rounds hit, the decision was unanimous. It was helmets and flak jackets and run like hell!"

Suydam and McDonnell, bare from the waist down but wearing their armor, ran for a bunker, while Walsh ran for shelter in another direction. "I was running like the devil for a bunker, hopping and skipping over the rocks in my bare feet, when I heard other Marines cheering me on," Walsh recalls. "I looked up and saw a group of guys in the doorway of the bunker shouting 'Don't stop! Don't stop! You've almost made it! Don't worry about your feet! Keep running!"

Diving into the bunker, Walsh was greeted by a round of applause and congratulations from his personal fan club. "I was standing there naked as a jaybird!"

Meanwhile, Suydam and McDonnell had arrived at the other bunker and leaped through the low entrance as enemy rounds erupted nearby. The men in the bunker had mixed expressions of shock and amusement, as they saw their commanding officer arrive, dressed only in his helmet and flak jacket. "They didn't seem to have any questions, though," the lieutenant recalls.

"In spite of the artillery and all, the hardest part of the whole episode was standing in the bunker, trying to hide behind a bar of soap," McDonnell contends.

**---- End of Gut and Glory Piece -----**

The contribution 2/1 made at Con Thien was re-engineering the whole place. When we arrived, the entrenchments and bunkers were in poor condition. We worked to rebuild the defenses and cleaned up the place so that it could withstand substantial attack if necessary.

*Before and after renovation at Con Thien.*

## Relieving the 26th Marines

The 26th Marines were surrounded
at Khe Sanh. The NVA intended to
cut them off, starve them, infiltrate
them and annihilate them. It was
part of General Giap's plan to
defeat the American forces in
Vietnam. By surrounding and
threatening to destroy the Marines
at Khe Sanh, he had hoped to draw
off significant resources leaving
the southern portion of the country
vulnerable to the countrywide
attack he planned for TET. As it
turned out, General Giap lost both
battles but won the war
nevertheless. The siege lasted for
ten weeks beginning January 21,
1968 and was declared officially
over April 5, 1968. The 6,000
Marines were surrounded by

20,000 North Vietnamese troops. Eventually, it became too dangerous to leave the base of operation. During the siege, the NVA fired more than 40,000 artillery, rocket and mortar rounds into the Marine positions. However, American air power dropped 80,000 tons of ordnance amounting to more than the non-nuclear tonnage dropped on Japan throughout WW II.

There were still plenty of enemy activity when we got involved. The east-west highway out to Khe Sanh is called Route Nine. It is a narrow winding road perched precariously on the side of a mountain range that dropped off into an east-west river valley, the Song Roa Quan. It was easy for the communist to disrupt traffic on the road. All you had to do was drop a hand grenade from the steep banks on the north side. The communist had cut the road to Khe Sanh with repeated ambush and the emplacement of troops. Without the only overland route to the base, there was no way to haul the heavy munitions necessary to keep the artillery batteries re-supplied. Air power was not suited for this kind of work. Without the road and the truck convoys of munitions, the batteries were effectively shut down thus allowing the encroachment of enemy forces toward the perimeter of the base.

*Photo of 155mm Self-Propelled Howitzer taken on Route 9. This one lane road with narrow bridges ran west to Laos and to the north turn at Kke Sahn. The track of this vehicle jumped the 4-inch guard rail rendering it immobile. They had to call for a jolly-green giant chopper to remove it. Efforts to camouflage the machine proved fruitless, so the Marines defiantly hoisted a rebel flag on the radio antenna.*

The joint Army, Marine operation to re-open Route Nine was called Operation Pegasus. On the sweep out to Khe Sanh, the First Air Cavalry Division took the south side of Route Nine; the First Marines (First Marine Regiment) took the north. As I recall, it took several weeks of mountain climbing and intermittent fighting to get there. The idea was to engage and destroy enemy units, to relieve the 26th Marines and to replace them with us, the Second Battalion, First Marines (2/1).

We believed that the Air Cavalry had it easy, flying from mountaintop to mountaintop each day while we Marines walked hill and dale. It seemed like we Marines always got the short end of the stick, the toughest assignments the worst supplies and equipment but I tell you that we wouldn't have had it any other way.

One of these hilltops was occupied and fortified. Our troops attacked it upon discovery, without waiting for orders. They just overran the place and killed all the bad guys. When the firing started, I started climbing forward. When I got to the top it was all over. One Marine said, "Look out for the trip wire." There it was about six inches off the ground. Several other Marines were disassembling the explosive. The mine was a Chinese Claymore called a Dinner Plate Mine. Molten TNT can be poured into any shape. This metal shape was round and about thirteen inches in diameter. It was four inches thick on the outside and shaped down to two inches in the middle. The backside was flat. While a round explosive energizes in all directions thus dissipating its force quickly like a light bulb, a shaped charge channels force in a single direction like the parabolic shaped headlamp of an automobile or flashlight. A pull friction fuse and explosive cap were found in the center of the mine. If exploded, it would have thrown shrapnel like a giant shotgun wherever it was aimed or in this case, along the trip wire.

We were going to destroy the mine by placing it in one of the bunkers, thus destroying the bunker in the process. The bunker roof was unusually heavy with at least a foot of timber, rocks and dirt. One Marine scoffed that the mine would not lift that roof. I said, "Yes it will." One pound of TNT will cut a railroad rail in two. A half-pound is sufficient to lift a roof off a bunker. The dinner plate mine had to have three pounds of TNT.   We argued back and forth.  When the mine exploded, I looked up to see logs and rocks twirling up about 30 feet in the air.  We were about 25 feet away from the bunker.  Then it began to rain logs and stones.  No one was hurt.  But, it was an impressive explosion and shower.

On one mountaintop, we were busy setting up our perimeter for night when there was a terrific explosion.  We all hit the dirt expecting the worst.  A little time passed.  Finally, someone said that a Marine was missing.  We began to search.  Eventually, we found his pistol, hot and twisted, and the thumb and forefinger of his right hand; that's all. I medevacked his remains with a note of identification. I placed the remains in one of those foil lined K-ration pouches. I've always wondered what the helicopter crew and the morgue thought about that. I have wanted to write to his family too. But, I can't even remember his name today. We believe that an 82-mm recoilless rifle killed him. These weapons fire a straight trajectory for miles. We never heard the report of a gun and there was no shell crater. Someone way off saw movement on our mountaintop and graced us with a shot. The round came screaming in just above ground level and impacted on this unfortunate Marine. Rest assured, he never knew what hit him.

When we arrived at Khe Sanh, I was amazed by the number of bomb craters and their proximity to the wire. The total landscape was pocked marked for miles with these enormous bomb craters. Also, there were enemy trench works dug out like blood vessels heading toward the wire. Many were close enough to throw grenades. The 26th Marines had only narrowly escaped annihilation and capture.

We were on a hilltop watching Marine helicopters come into Khe Sanh. One set down in a minefield. The first few troopers out of the chopper touched off a mine. The crew chief panicked, thinking they were taking incoming artillery and pushed all the Marines off the chopper. Five died. Another CH-46 was coming in and the prop wash blew up a poncho liner (like a blanket). It arced over and came in on top of the front rotor. The weight of the poncho liner in the prop caused the prop to become unstable and smash through the cockpit, killing the pilot and co-pilot.

Khe Sanh was a ghostly place with damaged aircraft bulldozed off to one side of the runway. CH-53 "Jolly Green Giant" helicopters would contour fly about 50 feet off the ground to Khe Sanh to avoid being seen by enemy artillery spotters. They would drop their under- slung net of cargo and depart just as artillery would come crashing in. We got a barrage nearly every time a chopper came in. One of the most heroic things I have ever seen was a black Marine driving a giant forklift machine. He would unload the landing zone (LZ) between artillery barrages. He was fast. When you heard the guns go off, you had about four seconds before the shells landed. As soon as the shells exploded, he would dash for his running machine and move cargo until he heard the guns. Then he would dive for cover.  What good were the supplies just delivered if they were to be destroyed by artillery in the LZ?

Although we spent ten weeks at Khe Sanh, we didn't seem to spend much time inside the perimeter. We went on many patrols and we sat on many mountaintops overlooking Khe Sanh.  We didn't want the enemy closing in on us again.

I recall one happy day when we were assigned demolition duty. There was a fortified Montagnard village just outside the gate of Khe Sanh.  Actually, I think it was the village of Khe Sanh, long since abandoned.   Intelligence was concerned that infiltrators and forward artillery observers were coming into that village and using the bunkers there for cover.  We took lots and lots of explosives, TNT. We would make up charges and then go destroy a bunker. By the way, a bunker is a hole in the ground with a roof made from logs and dirt. In one bunker we found a small cross bow, a decorative piece of cloth and two old swords. They were flimsy and rusty; probably used for ceremonial purposes. I have several photos as we staged sword-fighting scenes. Everybody got a kick out of this horseplay and wanted their picture taken.

*Me with cloth and sword.*

Another time, we were atop a ridge some distance from Khe Sanh. It was very dark, and I was walking along to get somewhere. Suddenly, Marines fired a 106-mm recoilless rifle. The shells for this weapon are as big as an artillery shell except the shell casing is perforated. This allows the expanding gasses to rush rearward from the weapon thus making it recoilless. The rearward rushing gasses go backward with such force that a man would be easily killed if he were in line with the gun and within fifty feet. Luckily, they were firing slightly down. I was about 20 feet directly behind the gun and the gasses passed over my head by about two feet. It sounded like a jet plane just missed me.

When we arrived at Khe Sanh, there were reportedly 7,000 enemy troops still operating in the area. During the next ten weeks, until the base was officially abandoned, US forces operating in and around the Khe Sanh base lost 400 KIA, and 2,300 wounded. These numbers were more than double the casualties sustained by the 26th Marines during the siege.

## Ambush of Fox-trot

We were at Khe Sanh.  Each day, a reinforced company with tanks would sweep the road for mines going south to LZ Stud about five miles to our rear. One morning, Fox company was ambushed during the mine sweep.  My skipper told me to go see Col. Duncan because the Fox-trot Company Commander had been killed and they needed a Company Commander. I was out of my mind with fear. When I got to Col. Duncan, I tried to tell him something that would dissuade him from sending me. I really did not feel up to the task. I was twenty-one years old, had flunked out of college, enlisted and commissioned through an enlisted commissioning program when I was twenty. I had to wait thirty days before leaving for Vietnam on my twenty-first birthday. I felt very comfortable leading a platoon, but a Company in combat? I was past scared. Col. Duncan stopped me after several words with......."I'm sure you'll do fine, Lieutenant." I had the last words,.......... ", Aye, aye Sir."

Echo 2/1 67-68 - Col Duncan & Lt Suydam

*It was an honor to serve in Col. Duncan's Battalion. He was a hell of a man and a brilliant combat officer.*

The fighting was over when I got there. The two M-80 tanks were burning. What a sight. They use an RPG-7 Rocket. It is a short metal tube with bamboo on the outside for a heat shield. The fins of the rocket fold up into the tube. The heavy large rocket explosive is outside of the tube. Our 3.5-inch rocket launcher held the whole rocket so it was large and heavy. Theirs has a percussion firing mechanism instead of the complex magneto of ours. Theirs required one man to fire. Ours required two. Like most of their weapons, they were simple and effective and could perform rings around ours. Even today, the Russian invented, Chinese made AK-47 is sought after because of its durability, effectiveness, ease of maintenance and killing power. I would choose the AK-47 over the M-16 any day of the week.

Hotel company had observed the ambush from a nearby mountain perch. They dropped down and closed in from the West thus trapping the remaining NVA soldiers between the two Marine rifle companies. A4 Sky Hawks were dropping napalm on the line between us. Each time they dropped the fire there was firing as the bad guys tried to run out. The Fox troops were demoralized and very happy to see me because I had bars, I guess. I was finally glad to have been given the assignment because of this. There was nothing for me to be afraid of and I felt that my just being there helped the others.

At the end of the day, we piled weapons (ours and theirs) on a duce-and-a-half truck with trailer. On top of the weapons, we piled dead Marines so high I thought the truck would tip over when it moved (about 20 Marines, I'm told). It was the saddest day of my life. The next day we were mopping up and captured two NVA survivors who were badly burned. They were young conscripts. It had been their first battle.

I had lunch with two Hotel Company Marines in June of 1999, thirty-one years after the facts. Carl King had been a platoon sergeant. Charlie Davis was a squad leader. It was wonderful to associate with these men and talk about the old days. I learned that on the day before the battle, Hotel was in a defensive perimeter on a hilltop overlooking the road. The road from Khe Sanh runs south from the combat base approximately 3-5 miles until it joins route 9. The communist infiltrated into the valley below Hotel Company between the hill and the road. During the night, they quietly dug fighting holes about 100 meters from the road and on the West Side. On the morning of the ambush, the enemy was completely hidden from Hotel Company by the early morning fog.

As Foxtrot Company came south with their mine sweep, a sapper came forward with a satchel charge that put the first tank out of commission. As the sapper retreated, Marines of Foxtrot chased him, unknowing that they were running directly into the enemy lines. This was the cause of the greatest loss of life. The second tank came alongside the first and was destroyed by a rocket. As the battle raged and the fog lifted, Hotel began to fire down on the enemy preventing them from retreating from their positions. With Marines on both sides, it made a perfect path for close air support to rain flaming death upon them. Enemy losses were significant, perhaps a hundred or more.

The Fighting for Hill 527.  April 21,
1968

Put your hand flat on the table and
then draw up your fingers and
your palm.  Now you have a hilltop
with fingers.  The fingers are
ridges that run to the valley floor.
Sometimes the fingers are long
and straight.  But, sometimes the
elevation drops off sharply at the
knuckle.  This was like the
mountainous terrain surrounding
the high valley of Khe Sanh.
Situated on the northwest
extremity of MacNamara's
Demilitarized Zone (DMZ), Khe

Sanh could be fired upon from Laos and North Vietnam. The 26th Marines at Khe Sanh had almost become America's Dien Bienphu. The French were surrounded in Dien Bienphu by the Viet Mien in 1954 and caused to surrender after a terrible siege. I'm told that France lost more men fighting in Vietnam (French Indochina) than did America.

I was the Executive Officer of Echo Company, 2nd Battalion, 1st Marines. Our mission at the time was to attack and reduce an anti-aircraft battery on Hill 527 that had been downing our planes. We had seen the Sky Hawks trailing smoke and pilots bailing out over Khe Sanh. The enemy was some distance from Khe Sanh otherwise we would have walked out to the fight. As it was, we planned a hellebore assault using the Marine workhorse, the CH-46 that carried about 9 Marines. The 46 had two equal sized rotor blades and a back door that let up and down for loading.

Hill 527 is seven kilometers due West of Khe Sanh, near the Laotian boarder. Perhaps you've heard of the Special Forces camp at Lang Vei that was overrun during the opening days of the battle of Khe Sahn. Hill 527 is about three kilometers north of Lang Vei.

My Captain was on Rest and Recuperation (R&R) in Australia, so I was acting Company Commander. I was called to a briefing. The assault would be two companies with Echo in the assault and Hotel in reserve. When I saw the map of the landing zone (LZ), I was horrified. The LZ was the only good-sized clearing and reasonably flat place for many kilometers in any direction. I felt that every enemy mortar and rocket for miles would be registered on this spot.

When I briefed my Platoon Leaders, I told them that the LZ would be hot. My instructions were for every man to get downhill and out of the LZ as soon as possible. I figured that men might not know north from east, but they surely would know down. The LZ was steep on the side of the mountain so that there was only one direction for down. I wanted no lolly-gagging in the LZ because I believed it would be a place of death. As it turned out, I was right.

Echo landed in two waves of six choppers. I was in the first wave. We dashed downhill almost falling and tumbling. As the second wave came in low for touchdown, I heard the mortars firing from the surrounding mountainsides. Dozens of mortar shells were in the air and arcing over to the LZ as the second wave touched down. The choppers were out and the LZ almost cleared as the LZ exploded with black smoke and earth. The third and fourth wave with the back-up company and Battalion Commander were waived off until air support could be brought to bear and quell some of the fire on the LZ. (I'm told by Charlie Davis in Houston Texas who was with Hotel Company, that he remembers the hot LZ. He states that Pfc. Strong was KIA and that Boykin and Cosnahan were wounded by mortar fire. When his Lt. Haaland asked to fire upon the mortars with 3.5-inch rockets, they were denied permission due to the proximity of Echo Company.) Actually, we weren't in proximity, but such was the fog of war.

The enemy anti-aircraft position was immediately in front of us, down the ravine and up the finger ridge in front.  It was the wrong way to approach the enemy and it would have been suicide.  We swung to the left and began to climb.  I wanted to swing the company around behind a hilltop that was between us and the objective and then attack down the finger ridge toward the enemy position.

A4 Sky Hawks were working the position with daisy-cutters.  These close air support bombs have enormous tail stabilizers that pop out to slow the bomb and eventually become part of the shrapnel.

We made our left flanking movement and used the terrain to shield our approach. The Battalion Commander, Lt. Col. Duncan, was on the radio now ordering me to swing right; to not go behind the hilltop. The top of the hill was a jurisdictional dividing line on the Colonel's map. By going to the left, we would be passing into another commander's territory and could be subjected to friendly fire. I deliberately disobeyed the order. Friendly fire was the least of my concern at the moment. All I wanted was an opportunity to line up our platoons under cover before releasing them in the assault. It worked perfectly. Sometimes I think the easiest job I ever had was being a Marine infantry officer. Marines don't need to be pushed. They only need to be held back until the critical moment. Once you release them, they know instinctively how to attack and pour fire on the enemy. They are energetic in the face of danger and ruthless killers in the heat of battle.

It only took a moment to line up. I called off the A4's and gave the order to attack. It was beautiful. It was textbook combat just like the exercises we practiced at Camp LeJeune and Quantico. It was probably the only time in Vietnam that I was involved in such a precision ground operation. My Marines charged into the enemy bunker complex like screaming hellions blasting everything in sight. We swept through in only a few moments. The enemy, already shaken by the A4's chose to skedaddle down the finger ridge and abandon the position. We found plenty of dead and plenty of blood spots indicating wounded.

Among the bunkers we found several doughnut shaped trenches that had been used for the anti-aircraft guns.

It occurs to me now that the enemy must have evacuated their anti-aircraft guns immediately. Otherwise they would have been brought to bear upon our choppers which were only 700-900 meters away across the chasm. Had this happened, many would have died in the Landing Zone.

Echo took no casualties that I can remember. I do regret the casualties suffered by Hotel Company in the hot LZ. Lt. Colonel Ducan forgave me for my temporary mutiny. He chalked it up to the fog of war and he put me in for the Bronze Star. It was one of the finest experiences of my life to command a company of Marines in combat and to be so successful in the mission.


The citation reads, (please take with grain of salt, these things are a little fluffy)

First Lieutenant Glen Lee Suydam, United States Marine Corps Reserve CITATION: For Meritorious service in connection with operations against the enemy in the Republic of Vietnam while serving in various capacities with Company E, Second Battalion, First Marines, First Marine Division from 23 June 1967 to 21 July 1968. Throughout this period, yatta, yatta, yatta, ..... On 21 April 1968, First Lieutenant Suydam's company was conducting a hellebore assault when the Marines suddenly came under a heavy volume of mortar fire from a large enemy force. Realizing the seriousness of the situation, he boldly maneuvered his unit against the hostile positions, shouting words of encouragement to his men (that one always gets me. Can you imagine such words?) and directing their fire until the enemy was forced to flee in panic and confusion. More yatta, yatta about being a goodie two shoes and helping out etc., in keeping with the highest traditions of the Marine Corps and of the United States Naval Service.

Lt. Wayne Haaland remembers the hot LZ near hill 527.

Hi

I enjoyed your account of Hill 527 although I'm not sure I even want to recharge forgotten issues. Let me add a little detail. I was Platoon

Commander of 2nd Platoon, Hotel Company. As usual, our platoon was the lead element for Hotel. I was the 4th man off the first helicopter, with Davis' squad. Like me, he always wanted to be in the lead. I was even upset that your unit got to go in first. You may remember that the helicopters were instructed in which direction to land and as I got off the helicopter, I luckily glanced at my compass and yelled for the point man to turn right as we were going in the wrong direction in relation to our first objective. Everybody turned and 10 seconds later our original path erupted in mortar explosions because the NVA shot a fire mission as soon as they determined the direction of the helicopter's offload. As we moved to our objective, we were exposed for a long time and our only cover was a series of bomb craters. We hop scotched from one to another until we finally reached cover.

Two interesting images come to mind during that scamper: (1) I watched an offloaded helicopter lift off with a reluctant warrior hanging from the ramp by his fingers. The crew captain stomped on his fingers until he dropped off from about six feet in the air. Even in that stressful moment, I had to chuckle at the one sane man on that mission. (2) Believe it or not, a tiger ran right past me and through our men; it was also trying to get out of the kill zone. He had evidently heard the gunfire and came looking for food, as they often did, but got there early. I questioned several men later and I think no one else saw this cat except me, although I am not surprised as like many other times, I had an overview of events and saw many things my men did not see because their view was squad or fire team oriented at best. Despite the terrible conditions, wherein we could not be anything other than targets for several heat strokes inviting hours (what genius dropped us off in the hottest part of the day?), the Marines did not panic, and we finally reached cover with minor casualties. Which is pretty amazing when you look back at the event, but I agree with you - they were terrific fighters and always followed orders - something that I rarely tried to do as usually the orders were stupid that came to me. We also discovered a bunker complex and destroyed it although it only had ammunition in it. Moments later, mortar explosions walked over the hill and wounded one or two of my men. I think it was friendly fire, but I did not say anything to my men as it stopped right after I yelled over the Battalion net to cease fire. We had to carry them out also. Kudos to you for your participation. I knew when we got the order of battle, as you did, that it was going to turn into a ridiculous mess.

Unfortunately, we were saddled with commanders who learned their lessons in Korea. They just did not understand the jungle. I would have blasted ten LZs to land in before we left Khe Sahn, and then I would have picked one at random - certainly not for its strategic position. I would also have put in a blocking unit in Laos to catch the bad guys when they headed out – but then what do I know?

Wayne Haaland

Ngo Van Tu

After Echo Company had secured Hill 527 outside of Khe Sanh by driving off the enemy from their anti-aircraft batteries, we set up a perimeter and began a search of the bunker complex. The account that follows has haunted me until this day and I tell it with such a mix of emotions that I cannot fully convey. The consolidation of the enemy's position was routine until I was informed that Marines had found a bunker entrance that was filled in with dirt. They were already digging into it when I got there.

Why fill in a bunker entrance with dirt? It took someone hours of backbreaking labor to dig the bunker by hand and cover it with logs, stone and earth.  To fill it in with dirt was pointless, unless.....................

More digging, then there were feet, jungle boots, US issue Jungle boots and stench.  The stench of rotting human flesh is overpowering and uncontrollably nauseating.  The rope around the ankles of the dead Marines had dug deep into their flesh.  Their hands were bound in front.  These two had been dragged from a battlefield, perhaps wounded but still alive to this place, perhaps tortured and finally after they died, thrown into this bunker grave and covered with dirt.  Why would you drag a dead Marine for miles up a mountain? No.  These Marines were taken alive.

We don't leave our wounded on the battlefield. We don't leave our dead in some forgotten Asian country to rot in an unmarked grave. This isn't written somewhere in a training manual. It's just part of the bond between fighting men. Even though we weren't taught it, we all believed it and were prepared to die in the effort to keep this commitment to our brethren. These two had become separated from their unit or perhaps their rescuers were killed in the struggle. The discovery of these bodies was both a blessing for their recovery and a haunting question as to how they could have been taken alive by the enemy and what horrors they endured before they died.

A historical note by Peter Brush brings into focus the horrors suffered by combatants at Khe

Sanh.  He writes in an article for Vietnam magazine:

"On February 25, a two-squad patrol, instructed not to venture farther than 1,000 meters from the base perimeter, vanished.  Two weeks later, casualties of the so-called ghost patrol were established as nine dead, 25 wounded and 19 missing.  A company-size patrol on March 30 had as one of its missions the recovery of the bodies of the ghost patrol.  This second patrol suffered three dead, 71 wounded and three missing before being ordered to pull back.  Only two bodies from the ghost patrol were recovered at that time."

Perhaps the bodies we found were from the ghost patrol or from the recovery party.  Their rings, watches, wallets and dog tags were gone...........souvenirs. I know this because I have taken the same from captured North Vietnamese Army (NVA) soldiers. It's what young combatants do when they have captured their enemy. But, the graves registration people would be able to identify these men from the list of missing in action and their dental records. Several began to wrap the bodies in rain ponchos and to secure them to carrying poles. Others were now opening marked graves around the bunker complex. The logic wasn't clear. If there were some dead Marines, then maybe there would be more. But, in the marked graves of the enemy? We weren't thinking clearly.

Several graves contained what we believe were Chinese judging from the enormous size of their bodies. The Vietnamese people are small.

One grave was marked with a cutout portion of a gallon tin can. I took it. It is one of the few souvenirs that I kept from the war. The soldier's name is Ngo Van Tu. His unit? U-40. This information is nail punched into the tin. But, the reason I kept the marker is because of what was on the back, which would have been the outside of the can. It reads, "Soybean Salad Oil, Donated by the People of the United States of America, Not to be sold or exchanged." There is a picture of hands shaking over a red, white and blue shield. I feel guilty to this day that because I took his marker, Ngo lies in an unmarked grave perhaps never to be identified for his family. I felt this guilt at the time, but I took it nevertheless. I didn't think that people would believe me without the souvenir. As it turned out, in the fifty years until today, I never have told anyone about it. It is hard to work these details into a conversation.

137

We couldn't leave the area from the LZ we had come into. It was hot and there wasn't another flat place for many miles. So, we began to walk........... up and down, up and down. The heat was unbearable. No one had to ask that the body carriers be relieved. We were going to return these honored dead to their mothers for proper burial and not a man among us flinched or shirked this duty in any manner. I couldn't have been more proud of these Marines.

Finally, we arrived at a place that could be used for a landing zone. It was like the knuckle of a finger, a grassy knoll that was just about big enough to call in a single chopper to take the bodies away. Our people were dragging with exhaustion and thirst. There are no streams of water in the mountaintops and our canteens were almost empty. The grass was head-high Elephant Grass. As the chopper waddled in trying to set down, a fire broke out in the grass and everyone in the LZ ran for their life. It was a hot, fast fire with flames reaching up twenty feet or more. We believe that the smoke grenade we used to mark the LZ for the chopper pilot to see from the air, started a small fire which was fanned into a roaring blaze by the prop wash of the chopper. A radio operator dashed up the hill with only the handset from his AN-PRC 25 radio. His radio and rifle burned to a crisp in the LZ. The bodies were smoldering. I watched with sadness as the fatigued young men of Echo Company poured their last dribble of their water onto the smoldering corpses. We wrapped them into

new ponchos and began anew
looking for an LZ and for water.

The LZ we sought now had to be
big enough to accept six choppers
at a time.  With two companies,
about 200 men, we had to load up
fast and get out before we could be
bracketed by artillery.  The
Battalion Executive Officer, Major
Wright, was directing me by radio
and binoculars from a mountain
top in the rear.  He ordered me to a
distant place that I thought
improbable.  I defied him.  I told
him his orders didn't make sense.
He got hot with me over the radio.
But, I could not understand the
logic of going to the place he
directed me to.  After he saw where
I was going, he called back and
apologized.  He said his map had
slipped in his map case and that
we were going to the right place
after all.

140

Somewhere in America, two mothers buried their missing sons. Echo Company had performed like champions. We were due some rest and relative safety before the next mission. It was time to clean weapons, read and write mail, bathe and cut each other's hair. Can you imagine? Inside the wire at the most exposed fire base on the DMZ was home and relative safety for these Marines.

Echo 2/1 67-68 - Shower Time

*Somebody invented a shower with an entrenching tool. This was Khe Sahn's water supply line. The base is to the left. The enemy side is to the front and right.*

In the last days of Khe Sanh, our orders were to demolish the defenses. The US had decided to abandon Khe Sanh. We cut open every sandbag, we filled in every trench and bunker, we ruined, wrecked and burned anything and everything of value. Toward the end, I was called away on Company business for three days. When I tried to return, I had difficulty getting back. There were no choppers going into Khe Sanh. Finally, when I did hitch a ride on a medivac chopper, I got off at a big clear spot in a valley that had once been our base of operation. There was a line of trucks about 200 meters away and believe me there was absolutely nothing else. I ran to them and found out that they were the last convoy leaving Khe Sanh. I climbed aboard the last truck. We rolled out cautiously, south to route nine and then east. The battles of Khe Sanh were over.

*Cpl. McKay and Gunny Lambert at work on destruction of Khe Sahn living quarters.*

We Marines didn't know it then, but American hope of winning in Vietnam was over too. Early in 1968, on the Vietnamese holiday, Tet, when the ARVN troops were all standing down from their duties, the communist launched a combined Viet Cong and NVA countrywide attack on South

Vietnam. It was the worst military defeat of communist forces ever suffered in the 87-year history of communist aggression anywhere in the world. The siege of Khe Sahn started just prior to TET, perhaps as a diversion for TET. During the heavily televised accounts of the communist defeats during TET and the siege of the 26th Marines at Khe Sanh, public sentiment in the US about obtaining victory in Vietnam slipped from slightly positive to slightly negative and would never recover. Even though American forces soundly defeated the maximum thrust of the enemy on a countrywide basis and the Marines had withstood and survived victoriously over the worst that the enemy could throw at them, America had lost its stomach for war in Southeast Asia.

The American public viewed the willingness of the communist to sustain unspeakable numbers of casualties as a threat they no longer wished to face because it meant a continuing stream of US casualties. In the years that followed, President Johnson announced that he would not run for reelection. Richard Nixon ran for President on a campaign promise to end the war. He was elected; he spent two more years seeking a victory, then he withdrew our troops leaving Vietnam to fall to communism.

May 22, 1999

Now that I've told everything that I can remember that's worth telling, I feel better. We vets didn't talk much about Vietnam. It was so unpopular, and nobody wanted to be reminded of the pain associated with the brother, sister, neighbor, uncle, father, husband or boyfriend that was ruined or lost. So, Vietnam era veterans mostly just kept quiet. This story telling all started when I found the 2nd Battalion, First Marine web page on the Internet. A few who had been where I had been swapped stories and before it was over, I had dredged up so many recollections that I wanted to write them down.

My brother-in-law asked me how it came to pass that I joined the Marines. I'll tell that story now.

I was born in 1946. I was probably one of the first baby boomers after WW II. My Dad served in the Coast Guard and did not go overseas. We kids grew up on cowboy movies and WW II films. Shows like Combat and Victory at Sea were popular on television. When we played, we played cowboys and Indians or war.

In high school, starting with the 10th grade, I joined the high school Reserve Officer Training Corps (ROTC). They gave me a uniform, a student rank and military job plus a rifle, an M1. Every young man in my day had by law, a six-year military obligation to satisfy. If he did not choose, then he would be subject to the draft. I liked the military stuff. I joined the drill team. We marched and paraded, we gave and took orders and we considered the possibility of a career in the US military.

I went to Auburn University as a freshman. Once again, I joined the ROTC. This was a more real situation. College graduates with four years of ROTC were guaranteed a commission if they went into service.

The Marine Corps had a program called the Platoon Leaders Course (PLC). It consisted of two boot camps, one after the freshman year and one after the junior year. I joined up. In the summer of 1965, I spent 10 weeks of boot camp at Quantico Virginia. I returned to college for the first quarter of my sophomore year, but I was not doing well. I had no direction or interest and my grades were failing. Having flunked out, I received a draft notice in a matter of weeks. As it was, I had already enlisted in the Marines and was on my way to Paris Island South Carolina. (I finished college after being discharged from the Marines.)

Paris Island boot camp was 8 weeks long followed by another 12 weeks of infantry training at Camp LeJuene North Carolina. With my previous training, I was a stand out. I was selected for an enlisted commissioning program. So, from infantry training I went to another boot camp at Quantico for ten weeks of Officer's Candidate School (OCS). Upon graduation, I was commissioned a 2nd Lieutenant and sent off to 26 weeks of The Basic School (TBS) at Quantico. TBS was intense training in tactics, logistics, map reading, military law and history, leadership, and command. My classmates were all college graduates including some from the Naval Academy. I graduated 56 in a class of 250. I was 176 pounds of twisted blue steel and sex appeal, we liked to say.

Upon graduation, I took leave and was to report from leave to San Francisco for a flight to Vietnam. At home, I received an extension of my leave. I was to ship out on my 21st birthday, June 29, 1967. I believe someone noticed that I was only 20 and did not want me in Vietnam as an officer at that age.

We flew a charter jet to Danang. On the way, we refueled at Wake Island (Could have been Midway). What an experience. From the air it looks like a dot in the Pacific. The Island is only a little bit longer than the runway and so narrow, you can see the surf lapping on both shores just by turning your head. There are only a few junky looking buildings there.

When we got to Da Nang, they put us into some barracks at the end of a runway. Jet planes took off over our heads all night.  Did they do that just to scare the hell out of us?  The next day we were put on trucks to take us to our respective units.  I can still remember that day like it was yesterday.  Never before or since have I seen such a deep lush green everywhere I looked, bamboo and rice.  Beautiful young girls walking to market with a duck and some vegetables to sell, squatted by the roadside to pee. When they smiled, their teeth were black surrounded by blood red, the indelible stain of the peasant narcotic chew, beetle nut.

There was one fellow on our truck whose uniform wasn't new and fresh like ours.  His was dirty, faded and tattered to shreds.  As we went along, there was a noise like a bumblebee passing quickly overhead.  This old salt immediately plastered himself to the floor of the truck. I remember feeling so sorry for him and how embarrassed he must have felt. I took me some days to realize that we had been shot at. Very soon, we all learned how to plaster ourselves upon the slightest provocation. This habit, once learned, was difficult to break after returning to the States, which led to further embarrassment back in the "world."

A few more stories and then I'm through with this, I swear. The first few weeks were difficult physically, the heat, the sweat, and the realization that you couldn't carry everything you wanted on your back all day, every day. Some things had to be discarded. For example, after struggling unsuccessfully with my Marine Corps skivvy drawers, one day, I just dropped my pants and cut them off with my bayonet. That way I didn't have to take off my boots. Anything that didn't do its job had to go. I didn't wear underwear again until I got back to Okinawa. And then it just didn't seem natural.

We were in a line walking along a dike crossing a rice paddy. We came to an intersection of dikes and the men in front of me were jumping across the intersection. It was all heavy with grass. I just didn't see the need to jump so I just walked through. It was an irrigation well. I splashed in over my head and had to be pulled out. I couldn't help thinking, what must my guys be saying? "Is this shave tail going to make it?"

The Headquarters and Service Company (H&S) manned the 2/1 perimeter at Phong Loc south of

Da Nang at night. Sometimes we'd return from patrol at night. We'd establish radio contact, ask permission to come in and then agree upon a visible signal such as a green star cluster (pop-up flair).

The troops were always a little indignant about the H&S "pogues" staying in the comfort of the wire. So, this one time, some old "salt" takes the green star cluster and shoots it level at the H&S bunker instead of up in the air. The H&S "pogoes" are manning a 50-caliber machine gun. Taking enormous umbrage to our offense, they open up on us. Actually, safely over our heads, but no matter, we still dive face-first into the paddy water. Are we scared? Yes, but at the same time, we're alternately laughing and cursing at the salt that shot the cluster. When no one was bleeding, it was all fun and games.

After the Union disaster at Fredericksburg Virginia in 1862 where Federal troops were slaughtered before the stonewall at Marye's heights, General Robert E. Lee remarked, "It's a good thing war is so terrible, otherwise we should grow fond of it." When I read this, I knew exactly what he meant. Vietnam, forgetting the bad things, was the most exhilarating experience of my life.

Echo 2/1 67-68 - Corporal Carter

*Cpl. Carter, company radio operator and entrance to command post at Con Thien, wearing NVA helmet.*

*Navy Corpsman, Doc Lynn, performs sanitary duty. This can is from a latrine and had to be burned with diesel fuel routinely.*

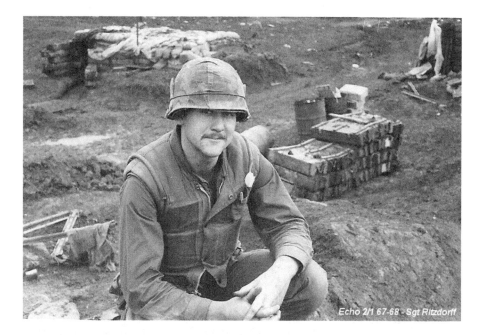

Echo 2/1 67-68 - Sgt Ritzdorff

*Sgt. Ritzdorff was a Squad Leader of the Third Platoon.*

*Second platoon leader, Lt. Graffam at Con Thien.*

Echo 2/1 67-68 - Corporal McKay

*Cpl. McKay. Some of the most exposed were Corpsmen who ran to danger and radio operators with the antennae overhead that said, "Here I am, shoot at me"*

Two 21-year-old youngsters, my hero, Dennis "Knobby," Knoblock (L) and me. We've seen each other twice in the last 50 years but we keep in touch.

-----THE END-----


------or, was it the beginning? -----

Made in the USA
Middletown, DE
30 August 2019